Alan Bates has been writing for a number of years now and his main area of interest is comedy and writing for stage and screen.

His work has been performed by the *English Touring Theatre* at *The Lyceum Theatre* in Crewe, and the author has recently trained in script writing at Keele University.

He has completed two full length stage plays to date, a comedy called *Lust in the Dust* and a dark psychological drama called *Platform 3*. He has also contributed to the late night ITV sketch show *Shoot the Writers*.

By day, Alan works in the printing industry, but is hoping to give the day job up in favour of his writing career.

THE POST BOX
AT THE CROSSROADS

Alan Bates

The Post Box
at the Crossroads

Vanguard Press

VANGUARD PAPERBACK

© Copyright 2005
Alan Bates

The right of Alan Bates to be identified as author of
this work has been asserted by him in accordance with the
Copyright, Designs and Patents Act 1988

A CIP catalogue record for this title is
available from the British Library
ISBN 1 84386 175 5

Vanguard Press is an imprint of
Pegasus Elliot MacKenzie Publishers Ltd.
www.pegasuspublishers.com

First Published in 2005

Vanguard Press
Sheraton House Castle Park
Cambridge England

Printed & Bound in Great Britain

To my dearest wife Frances who has stoically endured my eccentricities over many years.

And our lovely daughter Lorraine whose charm and wit illuminates our life.

Thank you to you both.

INTRODUCTION

I have devised an application technique for writing to people requesting something to which you are pretty sure they are going to say NO. It can be used for a job application, requesting a financial grant, asking someone famous to marry you, almost anything. The procedure is as follows. Firstly you write your letter of application. Then you wait for their refusal. You ignore that and write again saying that some catastrophic disaster has happened to the post box and your letter was destroyed. You post it off with a copy of your original letter. Their next letter usually reassures you that they have received your first letter but sympathetically reaffirms their refusal. You ignore this again and think up a more bizarre disaster that befalls the post box and send this off with another copy of your original letter. This process is continued for as long as necessary. I always start the letter off by saying almost apologetically, that disaster has struck. The post box which I always use (next to the off-licence, tanning studio and unisex hairdressers) has been the victim once again.

At about letter stage three, a number of things can happen depending on the humour or lack of it of the recipient. Some of them lose their sympathy and become almost aggressive. This type, at about letter number seven, lose their cool and sympathy completely. Some of them have become so exasperated that I have even had them sending me copies of letters of refusal that they have already sent to me. These people are usually no–hopers and it is unlikely that you will get anything out of them, so save your postage and try elsewhere.

The second type usually sees the joke and either offers you what you want or refers you to someone else. In fact I used this technique on one of our best loved comedy actors. Alas, he could not help me but sent me a very charming and encouraging letter which I treasure to this day. Also, I have to applaud his perception, as he noticed the wind–up straight away.

Finally, there is the third type who don't have any malice, but who realise that it is a wind–up and just ignore you. This last category should not be given up on because if you are imaginative enough they may look forward to your letters as it cheers up an otherwise dull day. And do bear in mind that they may be able to help you one day.

I always try to time the letters so that they arrive by first post, Monday. Hopefully, it gives the recipients something to look forward to when they come to work after a pleasant, or otherwise, weekend. Of course this does not work with the first category as they are probably made of wood anyway.

Something else to bear in mind is the technical accuracy of specialist information; or more accurately, inaccuracy of information. It sometimes pays dividends if you can make the odd yawning gaff, like for instance extolling the virtues of the fifteen–wheel arrangement of the 4-6-0 class of steam locomotives. This will get the hackles up of any self–respecting train spotter and they will be actually quivering with enthusiasm to correct you. Whether or not they will rise to the bait depends on which is stronger, the desire to ignore you or the desire to show off their knowledge and put the hapless clever–dick in his place.

I am using this technique at the moment, and at the time of writing I'm up to excuse number twenty–six, and no doubt by the time of publication it will be many more. Of course I can't say who I'm using it on as they may be reading this book. Anyway the first excuse follows. It is short and simple; I do think that this is the best policy when you start this process. When the prospective recipient gets the feel of it, or not, as the case may be, you can build up the momentum and size of the letter. But having said that, it does sometimes pay to put in the odd short letter to drop the victim down slightly. It does sometimes pay to 'treat em mean and keep 'em keen.' So, on with the first excuse.

Dear Sir/Madam,

I felt compelled to write to you again as disaster has struck. The post box, which I always use at the village crossroads (next to the off-licence, tanning studio and unisex hairdressers), has been the victim of a mindless arson attack by person or persons unknown. Alas, I fear my original letter to you was amongst the charred victims.

Apparently the blaze was spotted late last night by a group of Venezuelan philatelists, over here attending a prestigious stamp fair. They were on their way back from the Red Lion after sampling the heady and manifold delights of our native ale, of which each had imbibed about eight pints. It being an unseasonably cold evening and a good walk from the aforementioned hostelry, to their hotel the gentlemen were quite understandably in need of some relief.

Now here I must confess I must take my hat off to them, because they sprang into action, without a thought for their own personal safety, and tackled the blaze in quite a remarkable fashion. Now as I said, they were not a little uncomfortable in the groin area, and how shall I put it, they urgently needed to attend to the many calls of nature. Bearing this in mind and working in relays, they were able to contain the blaze and stop it spreading until the emergency services arrived.

Had the blaze spread to the off-licence, tanning studio and unisex hairdressers, well, the effect on the local community would have been too dire to contemplate; life would literally have come to a standstill. And as for the perpetrator of this terrible crime? Well, I have heard that a love–sick itinerant sheep shearer from Wogga Wogga is helping the police with their enquiries.

And so, because of those gentlemen's quick thinking and positive action, not to mention bravery, disaster was averted. We do indeed owe our Venezuelan friends a great debt of gratitude.

And for my original letter? Well I have enclosed a copy.

With my very best wishes to you,

Yours sincerely,

Dear Sir/Madam,

I felt compelled to write to you again as disaster has struck once more. The post box at the village crossroads (In front of the off-licence, unisex hairdressers and tanning centre) has been the victim yet again. I will explain the problem a little later as it involves our new vicar, whose first week in the village has been unusually traumatic.

His first professional engagement was a wedding, where I must admire him for keeping his cool against dire misfortune. The groom's granny was a trial to say the least. She was not a great advocate of personal hygiene and it was particularly warm in the church that day. Not only that, but she was a martyr to flatulence, usually interjecting at the more quiet moments, the church's excellent acoustics giving full vent to the effect. She was also the victim of a cold which had reached that uncomfortable catarrhal stage. More uncomfortable for the vicar as it happened.

Just after the "for better or worse" stage she let forth a stentorian sneeze; not only that, she let forth her top set which went spinning through the air, coming to rest like an obnoxious tiara on the vicar's head. Being new, his book "How to be a Vicar" did not cover uninvited head wear. So he carried on regardless.

As I mentioned she was not an advocate of hygiene and

this fact reflected itself in her dentures. Perhaps reflect is too strong a word as they were so discoloured they would not reflect anything. In fact, it is fair to say of the dentures that she only needed a white tooth and she would have had a snooker set.

Now the tiara with the remnants of a particularly mucous–laden sneeze were beginning to cause some anxiety as a trail of the catarrhal mucus was beginning to negotiate its journey down his forehead and around his nose. However he got through it with upright dignity.

The next day was Sunday and he was determined to put up a good show. Being new to the job he was advised (wrongly in my opinion) to have a small drink before going on, as it were. The small drink turned out to be four barley wines, the results of which on a man not used to it were interesting to, say the least. He had also been advised to hold something, such as a bible, for instance, so giving his nervous hands something to do.

Now here I fail to understand his reasoning. I can only assume that it was the effects of the alcohol, as he stood in the pulpit, not with a bible but with a ventriloquist's dummy. Actually he was quite an accomplished performer. Bleary–eyed at the end of the service, he bade the congregation farewell at the church door. One crusty old parishioner told him in no uncertain terms that his sermon was rubbish, but that the little guy had a promising future.

The bishop had also been present to witness his inaugural sermon and had these wise words of advice: "I think in future, my son, it would be more in keeping with the traditions of the church if you said that David slew Goliath instead of saying he kicked the crap out of him."

The following day he was to encounter a further dilemma. The problem this time was low–flying aircraft. Now I know these young fighter pilots have to do their training in realistic circumstances. They have to be able to fly their little planes at twice the speed of sound, in the dark, six inches above the ground and in a blizzard. Well on this fateful day, the vicar was but fifty yards from the post box and bent down to tie his shoelaces (there was a freak blizzard at the time I believe) when a plane of unknown origin flew up the main street of the village. The startled vicar found himself sitting astride the nose of the plane. The even more startled pilot took emergency action, pulled back on the stick and climbed to a great altitude. This caused the vicar to start sliding down the fuselage. One can only wonder at the thoughts racing through the pilot's mind as an unidentified crutch in grey pin stripes slowly approached and passed over his cockpit canopy, followed by the sad face of a vicar pressed against the glass by mach one airspeed, leaving an unsightly trail of saliva on the glass.

The poor vicar slid all along to the tail section, and there he sat leaning on the rudder at the back of the tailplane quite 'happily' (or perhaps happily is putting it a bit strong) while the pilot thought out what to do next. The only course of action was to go into a gentle dive. This caused the vicar to slide towards the cockpit. I am happy to say that the quick–thinking pilot opened the canopy and pulled him inside to safety.

They landed at the air base and the vicar was revived with whisky and hot sweet tea in the officer's mess.

The vicar for his part was uplifted by the experience, being taken closer to God, so to speak, and no doubt had unique material for next Sunday's sermon. But alas, during the adventure, the plane clipped the post box, knocking it over. The sudden ascent of the plane and the combustible effects of its afterburner rendered the contents of the post box a pile of cinders. I fear my letter to you was amongst the victims.

But fear not, I have a copy and please find it enclosed herewith. And as for the post box at the village crossroads (next to the off-licence, unisex hairdressers and tanning centre) well, it has been replaced.

With my very best wishes to you,

Yours sincerely,

Dear Sir/Madam,

I felt compelled to write to you again as disaster has struck once more. The post box at the crossroads (in front of the off–licence, unisex hairdressers and tanning centre has been the victim yet again.) A few days ago a convoy of lorries containing nuclear material passed through the village. Unfortunately one of them failed to negotiate the crossroads. It rolled over on to its side and spilled a quantity of its atomic cargo, which, as you have probably guessed, contaminated the post box at the crossroads. Fortunately there was no danger to life, and I have to take my hat off to the emergency services who reacted quickly and efficiently. The post box was immediately encapsulated in concrete to make it safe. And here I have to congratulate the concrete company, both for their rapid response to a potentially catastrophic accident and for their artistic taste. Rather than leave the concrete encapsulation as a shapeless monolith, they modelled the top into a bust of the Reverend Timothy Martinwood from Macclesfield, a man who had no connection with the village whatsoever, but who was an ancestor of the proprietor of the Acme Concrete and Garden Gnome Company.

Now for my part, Macclesfield has always been a place of some mystery. Until this nuclear incident I never knew what a maccle was, only that there was a field full of them in Macclesfield. The popularity of the maccle, which presumably is some small furry creature, was championed by the previously mentioned nineteenth century clergyman the Dean of Macclesfield, the Reverend Timothy Martinwood. A man apparently internationally famous for his studies on both the common maccle and the lesser grey maccle. Unfortunately, the maccle it is said, only breeds during periods of high sunspot activity. Because of this I am told that both species of the maccle have all but become extinct. A sad story indeed and the Reverend Martinwood died in obscurity, a broken man, the only love of his life also in obscurity. I feel sure that those of us with certain religious convictions know that in the great somewhere Timothy Martinwood and his maccles, both the common and the lesser grey are at last reunited. Let us hope so.

Alas, there stands the post box and the Rev. Timothy Martinwood, and my letter to you, intact, but sealed within. But let us not be downhearted because even as I write a new post box is being erected next to the monument. And what about the letter? I hear you ask. Fear not, I have a copy and please find it enclosed herewith.

With very best wishes to you,

Yours sincerely,

Dear Sir/Madam,

I felt compelled to write to you again as disaster has struck once more. The post box at the village crossroads (in front of the off-licence, unisex hairdressers and tanning centre) has been the victim yet again. It has, as you may have guessed, been the subject of yet another incident. In short it is no longer there. Apparently, during the night the post box was the centre of a religious celebration. It is said the site which it occupies was many years ago, and to some latter day followers, still is, a sacred spot. It was here that the tenth century B.C. prophet Jethro the Incandescent died, and legend has it that he immediately ascended skyward at great velocity. In keeping with the legend the post box has done the same. To mark the anniversary of his ascension, the latter day followers of jethro the incandescent strapped home-made rockets to the post box and launched it into space. It is now in geosynchronous orbit somewhere above the Indian Ocean. This unauthorised launch has obviously had potentially serious repercussions. An international state of war readiness was caused, as each superpower believed the other was launching a pre-emptive strike. Needless to say, the respective hot lines were very hot indeed as each super power emphasised its non aggression.

The post box will obviously come down, and its re-entry was recently calculated by the eminent Professor Ignacious Crowe, Professor of Difficult Sums at a university whose name escapes me. The rate of decay of its orbit has been calculated at six years, three months and twelve days and it is expected to come down somewhere in the Urals.

There was speculation of a joint Anglo–American rescue plan, but due to budget cuts this plan has been abandoned. It appears that safe and complete recovery is impossible. Post boxes, alas, have not been designed to withstand the trauma of orbital re-entry, so we must fear the worst. NASA has agreed to keep me informed of its progress. On a happier note, however, I am pleased to say that the departed post box has been replaced with a brand new one. I shall of course keep you informed of its adventures. And for my original letter, well I have enclosed a copy.

With my very best wishes to you,

Yours sincerely,

Dear Sir/Madam,

I felt compelled to write to you again as disaster has struck once more. The post box, which I always use at the village crossroads (in front of the off-licence, unisex hairdressers and tanning centre) has been the victim of yet another incident. This time it was a flood, a flood of unimaginable proportions. But perhaps I am being too damning, as it was not the flood itself but the results of it that were the problem. Allow me to explain.

Now the flood, contrary to what you would expect was not the result of freak weather but of bureaucracy at its most incompetent. A dam had been built without prior consultation with the people of the village with the consequence that the village crossroads would become submerged much in the manner of Abu Simbel. Naturally the residents objected, but to no avail, the powers that be were adamant that the project would go ahead, and go ahead it did. An action committee was formed and its unanimous resolve was that WE SHALL NOT BE MOVED. And moved we were not.

Eventually the fateful day arrived and the water levels rose. The blitz camaraderie was rock–solid and the community prepared for life under water; motor vehicles were adapted for this new and alien environment, sub–aqua equipment replaced the umbrella and shoes were replaced by flippers.

A sort of adapted normality pervaded the folk of the village. I would not say everything was as it would be liked. For instance the sparrows and black birds were coping quite well but I have to say the starlings were finding flying under water a little irksome. Another problem for our ever troubled feathered friends was the fact that now the cats could move in three dimensions. Not that this was really a great problem for the birds because although the cats were more mobile they were also slower, so the status quo was more or less maintained.

A bigger problem for the birds, indeed for everyone, was fish. Fish of all sizes. Some very small and some quite monstrous, one in particular is the subject of my problem and I will come to that in a moment. One of our tribulations in the dry days was ants. Now, however, you are likely to put your slippers on in the morning only to find a rainbow trout asleep there. Wash day bought its own set of problems and clothes hung out on the line never really had that crisp dry feel to them. But we got by.

Now the previously mentioned aquatic monster was a huge thirteen–foot pike. Well, one morning Bert, our intrepid post man with his smart Post Office issue scuba gear, was going to collect the mail from the post box (at the village crossroads in front of the off-licence, unisex hairdressers and tanning centre) when the unimaginable happened. He collected the mail into his sack and was set upon by the huge pike. Bert fought bravely, slashing the monster repeatedly with his sack. The enraged beast lunged at Bert once more, luckily he dived out of the way and the pike struck its head on the post box. Quick as a flash, Bert rammed the sack into the pike's mouth and reached for his spear gun. How fortunate that the postal employers have not only trained their staff to deal with savage dogs but also their marine equivalents.

Unfortunately, in that brief moment the pike had swallowed the mail sack and with a satisfied burp swam on its way. I have to say that in the sack was the manuscript of my wife's latest novel, my latest stage play and, yes, you've guessed it, my letter to you. I can only think of that great fish digesting the writings. As we consider the events let us spare a thought for Bert and, indeed, for the fish and what he ate, and let us be grateful that our piscatorial friends are taking an interest in literature and the performing arts.

I am now happy to report that the flooding debacle has been resolved. Apparently the dam project had somehow landed in the wrong in-tray of whoever deals with these matters. The plans were for a dam project in some remote part of India and had got mixed up with plans for the crossroads. But apparently the villagers of that remote, arid, little mountain village are very pleased with their new bus shelter.

I am glad to report that the flood waters have now gone and so has the pike. And what of my original letter to you? Fear not, a copy is enclosed herewith. With my very best wishes,

Yours sincerely,

Dear Sir/Madam,

I felt compelled to write to you again as disaster has struck once more. The post box, which I always use at the village crossroads (in front of the off-licence, unisex hairdressers and tanning centre) has been the victim of yet another incident. In fact what happened was truly unbelievable. I walked to the post box and posted my letter, turned to walk away and as I did so I heard an angelic voice calling my name. Looking around I could see no one, not only no one but no traffic or birds or anything. The crossroads were still and silent. I thought, well, it's one of those rare occasions when there is a pause in the traffic. I waited, but nothing; I stood in the middle of the road and looked up and down, but nothing. This was slightly scary. Then I remembered I saw old Joe go into the off-licence. I looked through the window and there he was handing his money to Sheila. But they weren't moving, they were like two statues. I'll go in, I thought, and see what's going on, but the door would not open. It can't be locked so why won't it open? I hammered on the glass to attract their attention but it didn't make a noise. Have I gone deaf? I thought, but no, I had coins in my pocket and I could hear them. Then the angelic voice called my name again, it was coming from the post box. I stood transfixed as a blue iridescent smoke came out of the letter slot and surrounded my feet. It rose up around me until it was up to my chest. It felt strange a sort of warming electrical feeling, if that makes sense. The level of the smoke continued to rise until it covered my face and head. My instinct was to move away but I was fixed to the spot. I'm going to be suffocated by the smoke, I thought, but to my surprise I found I could breathe quite easily and I felt cleansed. The smoke engulfed me for a few seconds then started to subside; as it descended I could see that it was going back into the letter slot. Eventually it had all gone. The silence and stillness still pervaded the crossroads.

Then the door opened on the post box and inside was the blue smoke with a strong light shining through it. The voice called to me again and I felt myself being drawn in. I got inside the post box and the door closed behind me. Through the blue mist I could see someone approaching. It was a beautiful woman dressed in a white figure–hugging robe with a cord around her waist. "I am Wanda," she said, "and I am from the inner world."
"How may I help you?" I said, rather unoriginally.
"Our people are sick and need your help."
"But how can I help? I have no medical knowledge."
"The answer is simple. We need just a little protein for our diet and all will be well. Just a small amount and that will nourish us for another hundred years. Will you help?"
"I'll do what I can."
"Thank you."
And with that she walked back into the blue mist.
The door opened and I was in daylight again. But what am I to do about the protein? I walked along the road to the supermarket where, sure enough, time was still standing still, people like statues. To my great good fortune they were receiving a delivery of steak pies, the delivery man with a tray full on his shoulder. I relieved him of his tray and placed in his hand what I estimated was suitable

28

financial recompense. Boy, is he going to be surprised when he wakes up, I thought. I hurried back to the post box with the pies.

I stood there with my tray and coughed. I felt rather foolish but I thought, how else do I attract attention? Anyway, my cough worked and the post box door slowly opened to reveal the familiar blue haze. I stepped inside and the beautiful girl came to meet me.

"You have returned," she said, "and you have bought us protein. We thank you."

A young boy emerged from the mist and took the pies.

"We will be eternally grateful to you."

"But who are you? Where are you from?" I asked.

"We live down below the earth. Our lives are simple, pleasurable and long. We have no disease or anti–social behaviour; we simply live to give ourselves pleasure. Why do you not join us? I need one such as you and I will give you pleasure."

"Can I think about it?" I said.

"I must know now, I have to return to my people with the protein."

I was sorely tempted but declined. Disappointed, she bade me farewell and disappeared into the blue mist.

The door opened and I was in daylight again. The post box descended into the ground, I looked down into the blackness but could see nothing. A few minutes later it reappeared. Then things came back to normal. Old Joe emerged with his beer and regaled me for five minutes, complaining about the price of ale. The traffic was moving and a delivery man drove past with a handful of money and a puzzled look on his face. And imagine Bert's face when he came to empty the post box only to find a load of foil pie trays but, alas, no letters.

But not to worry, I have a copy and please find it enclosed herewith.

With my very best wishes,

Yours sincerely,

Dear Sir/Madam,

I felt compelled to write to you again as disaster has struck once more. The post box, which I always use at the village crossroads (in front of the off-licence, unisex hairdressers and tanning centre) has been the victim of yet another incident. I had posted my letter last night and had missed the evening collection. To my surprise this morning whilst walking towards the crossroads I was met by a very distressed Bert the postman. Apparently he was unable to empty the box because of a political demonstration. Members of the popular front of the village had climbed onto the roof of the post box and, using a loud hailer, were making political demands. Their most forceful and audible was for autonomy for the village. They wanted their own government and full independence and had also made demands for money for their armed forces. Now this armed forces nonsense was, I must admit, a bit of a worry, as they had made inroads into building up a three–service force already. At the moment it was at the early stages, but worrying nevertheless. So far they had infiltrated the scouts and girl guides movement, distributing revolutionary media and setting up training camps. The village is justifiably proud of its lake but the popular front has established the nucleus of a Navy, consisting of a formidable surface fleet of oil drum class frigates and an undisclosed submarine fleet. Undisclosed because they have never surfaced. It could be nothing, but who knows? it could be the ultimate something or other. More worrying still is the unusual activities of the seemingly innocent local gliding club, with their aircraft soaring overhead with suspicious projectiles on their wings. It may be nothing again but the feeling locally is that this movement should be nipped in the bud.

Now back to the post box. As I say, the group had established themselves on the roof of the post box and they were determined in their cause and would stop at nothing. Ultimately they would rather die than give in, and if their hand was forced they would all throw themselves, women and children too, off the top of the post box to certain death and martyrdom. To this end the authorities had positioned safety nets around the bottom of the post box. This was to be a hazardous and time–consuming exercise as the demonstrators were hurling bricks and other missiles down at anyone who approached.

Even a police helicopter that was circling high up around the top of the post box came under attack from withering catapult and water–pistol fire and had to retreat to a safer distance to avoid being shot down. The demonstrators held all the cards. They had sufficient provisions for many days and more importantly, they had caught the attention of the world's media and had gained sympathy and support from other fringe political movements. It had the potential of escalating into world wide anarchy. The problem was serious.

The crossroads were cordoned off and the waiting game began. Almost continually the demonstrators' megaphone barked out their political dogma. No one could sleep. Their leader was one Brenda Goodthighs, a force to be reckoned with, a woman so powerful that even skinheads crossed the road to avoid her.

It was Bert the postman who eventually came up with the solution. Now Brenda's mail had been intercepted by the security forces for surveillance purposes and it transpired that she had won a competition at a local supermarket, the prize being a car in the colour of the winner's choice and a unique trolley dash around the store in the said car. Brenda's car in customised camouflage paintwork was ready for her collection. Now Bert knew she was a shopaholic and suggested a face–saving solution. If they gave up the sit in, it was agreed that the village should have a special stamp printed with Brenda's profile on it and that dialogue with the authorities could commence. That would allow them to give up with honour, Brenda would have her new staff car and she would be able to completely re-supply her organisation, paid for by the supermarket.

The proposition was agreed and the demonstration was over. Scaffolding was erected and the demonstrators descended with dignity and applause. Everyone was relieved at the outcome. Now Bert could continue with his collection, but as a high percentage of the demonstrators were women with young babies, it appeared that the nappies were disposed of in not a very considerate manner. They were in fact posted through the letter slot, and damage was done. I am afraid my letter was one of the victims. But fear not, I have a copy and please find it enclosed herewith.

With my very best wishes to you,

Yours sincerely,

Dear Sir/Madam,

I felt compelled to write to you again as disaster has struck once more. The post box, which I always use at the village crossroads (in front of the off-licence, unisex hairdressers and tanning centre) has been the victim of yet another incident. The problem this time was that noble beast of the Serengeti, the wildebeest. 120,358 of them, to be precise, plus one zebra with an identity crisis.

The village awoke one lazy, sunny Sunday morning to a vista of grazing animals as far as the eye could see. Everyone was baffled. Why were they here? Where had they come from, and how? The theory put forward was that they were on their annual migration and word got around the herd that lions were lying in wait. Now the herd had a new leader called Spartacus and he had decided that the wildebeest was going to be the fall guy no more. He had a stunning plan. He was going to sort out these loud-mouthed lions once and for all. He decided to deviate from their normal route and come up behind the lions and catch them unaware and give them a thrashing that they would never forget.

Unfortunately, Spartacus was a better talker than he was a navigator and so he and 120,357 of his chums plus one zebra found themselves at the village crossroads (in front of the off-licence, unisex hairdressers and tanning centre). Spartacus was not a little embarrassed, but in time the herd found friends among the community and fitted in quite well. Not all was sweetness and light, however. His brother, Bruno, disappointed at not having the punch–up with the lions, and despairing at Spartacus' zero navigation skills, wanted out. In short, he was trouble.

What of the people of the village? I hear you ask. Well it was a mixed blessing. To some it was a nightmare, as traffic through the village was bought to a virtual standstill. The film and television crews were also a source of some friction. But the world wanted to hear and see this unusual occurrence. But to others the constant microphone being pushed in your face and being asked, "How has the wildebeest affected your life?" was too much to bear, and many a reporter has walked away from an irate villager with teetering steps and a microphone inserted between his buttocks.

But let us not be all negative, as a new wave of entrepreneurs have emerged. The wildebeest, as with all living things, consume and shall, we say, deposit. And so was born the manure magnate. overnight millionaires selling the fertile efforts countrywide and indeed, in some cases, exporting. They have, in financial parlance, 'cleaned up', literally and figuratively.

Back to Bruno. He longed for the Serengeti as village life did not suit him at all, and he had been in long discussions with the village committee, many of which wanted the immigrants returning to their homeland. A deal had been struck. The only person to get them home was Fatima the queen of the elusive Fakhawi tribe, a nomadic people of small stature who lived in the savannah grasslands. Very few people had seen the Fakhawi due to their somewhat diminutive size and their desire to live in long grass. The story has it that they wore long feathers on their heads and as the sun was setting these feathers could be seen as the lost tribe jumped up and down in the long grass chanting their tribal call of, "we're the Fakhawi, we're the Fakhawi."

Anyway, Fatima was found, and agreed to take the animals back home. It was a magnificent sight as she led them through the crossroads (in front of the off-licence, unisex hairdressers and tanning centre) like a modern day Pied Piper of Hamlin. Eventually all had gone, bar one Spartacus. He stood defiantly in the middle of the crossroads. He wanted to go but he also wanted to lead and he had a score to settle with Bruno and the lions. In a fit of temper he demolished the post box (in front of the off-licence, unisex hairdressers and tanning centre) and trampled the mail within. An act of extreme petulance I thought. He then ran after the herd, barging his way to the front so he could lead.

So the episode was over and the village reverted back to normality. The post box was replaced but, as you may have guessed, my letter to you was lost during Spartacus' tantrum.

But fear not, I have a copy and it is enclosed herewith.

With my very best wishes to you,

Yours sincerely,

Dear Sir/Madam,

I felt compelled to write to you again as disaster has struck once more. The post box, which I always use at the village crossroads (in front of the off-licence, unisex hairdressers and tanning centre) has been the victim of yet another incident. Or to be more precise, it wasn't so much a problem with the post box, but rather with Bert, our intrepid postman. As I approached the post box there was Bert, looking far from his chirpy self and not only that, he was emptying his sandwich box into a nearby bin. Now I had seen him do this on a number of occasions recently and detesting the wasting of good food, I decided to tackle him about the waste and his long face. He began his tale of woe of which I shall relate.

Apparently he had fallen out with his wife again and he was now living with his auntie, a situation which was far from ideal, the reasons for which I will explain in a moment. Now for the split with his wife I have to blame them both equally. There had been friction for some time because of their different backgrounds, his wife Elizabeth had come from a very upper middle class background and had pots of money. Her parents were both very successful in the City and they disapproved of Bert. Everything was against him, even his name, which summed up his character and his background. Bert and Elizabeth just didn't, in their eyes, go together. And his occupation, a lowly postman. Elizabeth's forebears could be traced back three hundred years and there was even the faintest connection to an earldom. Bert's father was a sagger maker's bottom knocker (yes they do exist), as was his father before him. There was no denying that Bert felt a little ill–at–ease, but he liked his job, it was honest labour and although he was not proud of his heritage, there was little he could do about it.

Bert was reading the local paper one evening and came across a matchmaking section and decided to put an advert in it. He over–glamorised himself a little, I think, as he described himself as having the grace of a Caribbean stallion, which in truth was the name of a horse that won the 3.15 and earned him £20. His luck was in and he had a reply from a seductive sensitive siren. He wrote back and a rendezvous was arranged. Not a successful evening I have to say, the siren that met the Caribbean stallion was non other than Elizabeth, his wife. Neither was very pleased. For one thing, Elizabeth's idea of a Caribbean stallion was someone tall, dark, and shall we say, athletic. And as for her description as a siren, well I've met her and I think foghorn is probably nearer the mark.

Now that is why he is living with his auntie, a woman who, for want of a better description, has not come to terms with personal hygiene. To cheer Bert up she made him a beautiful steak and kidney pie which he ate with relish. Bert loved pies and it was his habit of eating the filling first and saving the pastry till last. This he did and when he scraped the last morsel of gravy off with his knife to his horror in the pastry was a row of parrot's foot prints. Apparently auntie kept a huge free–range parrot that had the run off the house and had obviously put his personal stamp on the pie. His favourite perch was the light fitting in the middle of the room and from this vantage point he could decorate the trifle below.

I am happy to say that Bert is attempting a reconciliation with his wife before he starves to death. And how has this episode affected my postal communication? I hear you ask. Well, when I addressed and stamped the envelope I realised that the flap had no gum on it, and not having any in the house, I stuck it down with marmalade. Unfortunately during his lunch break Bert took his postal collection into his auntie's and the parrot, detecting the marmalade, ate the letter. But fear not, I have a copy and please find it enclosed herewith.

With my very best wishes to you,

Yours sincerely,

Dear Sir/Madam,

I felt compelled to write to you again as disaster has struck once more. The post box, which I always use at the village crossroads (in front of the off-licence, unisex hairdressers and tanning centre) has been the victim of yet another incident. A few days ago, Bert the postman was going about his legitimate business of collecting the mail when he was thrust into a nightmare scenario. It was quiet as usual, as people went about their business, when, in the distance was the unmistakable whine of police cars. They seemed to be in hot pursuit of a blue van that was being driven erratically. As Bert opened the post box his attention was seized by the sound of screeching tyres and the distinctive sound of blue van on parked car.

Three masked and armed men dived out of the now un-road-worthy vehicle. Five police cars came also to an abrupt and screeching halt and about twenty armed police officers continued the chase on foot. The pursued, now in panic and not having a line of escape headed in Bert's direction. He was seized by the terrorists and was forced at gun–point into the post box. The terrorists also got in and slammed the door shut, locking it from the inside. The post box was immediately surrounded by the armed police, who took up positions of cover.

A tense, and foreboding atmosphere descended as lengthy but fruitless negotiations then ensued. Demands for the release of political prisoners and a safe passage out of the village were made and refused. Tension was running high, especially for Bert's wife as his tea was in the oven and she needed his car keys to go to aerobics. The terrorists had strengthened their position to a formidable strategic advantage. They had loosened the base of the post box and it now revolved like a turret giving them unlimited fire power in all directions. They were in command of the crossroads, and they were bullet proof.

Night descended. The terrorists had access to a powerful searchlight as well as their formidable armoury and periodically the searching beam would sweep across the crossroads like an ominous and terrifying light house. Anything or anyone caught in the beam was immediately fired upon. Throughout the first night sporadic gun fire came from the letter slot of the post box, just to prove that they were forever vigilant. Eventually, after many days of fruitless talking and bargaining, negotiations broke down and fearing the worst, the SAS were summoned from their secret HQ in Herefordshire.

Picture the scene if you will. It was early morning, the sun was just rising, and there was an almost audible silence, except for faint snoring coming from the post box. The terrorists, and Bert also no doubt, had, after many days of stress and tension, finally succumbed to sleep. A lone figure crept silently upon the post box and attached a cable to the door. Silence. Then in the distance could be heard the faint but unmistakable beat beat–beat–of a helicopter. In a few minutes the helicopter was over the post box in a stationary hover. Five ropes descended, and then a squadron of SAS troops silently abseiled down. They mustered on the roof of the post box. A signal was given and in through the letter slot stun and gas grenades were thrown. Simultaneously, a truck sped away, pulling off the post box door. Immediately the SAS slid down their ropes and the five of them stormed the post box guns, blazing. There was shouting and shooting and the sound of explosions as the grenades went off. The noise and confusion seemed to be going on for an age, but probably in reality it was all over in seconds. An eerie silence fell again. Then, a moment later, out of the smoke emerged the terrorists, hands held high. They were immediately seized and arrested by the waiting police. To the SAS, for their part, well, it was just another day and another mission successfully accomplished, and they were picked up by the helicopter and whisked back to base for debriefing. They have our heartfelt thanks.

Thankfully the episode was over without loss of life and good triumphed over evil. Bert was reunited with his family. The terrorists are now serving a long stretch in one of our excellent prisons. Alas, as you can probably appreciate, the siege going on for several days, and the post box having no heating or toilet arrangements, well I fear human shortcomings took their toll and my letter was lost in the confusion.

And for my original letter? Well I have enclosed a copy, digitally saved in my computer. How fortunate.

With very best wishes to you,

Yours sincerely,

Dear Sir/Madam,

I felt compelled to write to you again as disaster has struck once more. The post box, which I always use at the village crossroads (in front of the off-licence, unisex hairdressers and tanning centre) has been the victim of yet another incident. Or to be more precise, Bert has been the victim of another incident. Poor old Bert has been in the wars again and little knowing that he was going to end the day with two broken legs. He had done his usual collection and had got talking to Dave, his old drinking partner. Dave was a pleasant bloke but a bit simple and had just got married again for the seventh time, which gives some measure of his stature. He was in something of a flap because of a domestic crisis, a plumbing crisis to be exact. Bert, being something of a handy man, offered to help, the offer was gratefully accepted and they both went to Dave's flat.

After walking up countless flights of stairs, due to the mechanical breakdown of the lift, they arrived a little breathless at Dave's flat. Dave went for his tools and Bert got under the kitchen sink to turn off the stop cock. Unbeknown to him Dave's new bride came in with the shopping and put it on the table. Seeing a man bending down under the sink she quite naturally, assumed it was Dave and also quite naturally being recently married and still in the full flush of adventure, so to speak she, how shall I put it, she grasped him intimately. The sudden shock made Bert jump up and bang his head on the bottom the sink, rendering him unconscious.

How did this cause two broken legs, I hear you ask. Well, the paramedics were summoned and Bert was stretchered away. Unfortunately as they were carrying him out they were laughing so much from the story of his concussion that they dropped him down several flights of stairs. Still being unconscious he was spared the pain of multiple fractures. Being the professional that he was, all through the plastering process he insisted on keeping his collection with him until an authorised person could relieve him of it. Now unfortunately, and I don't know how this happened, my letter to you became amalgamated with the plaster on one of his legs. It could just be seen tantalizingly close to the surface, but the plaster had set and unfortunately there it had to remain.

Bert made good progress and was soon home. His home is large and stately, a legacy from his wife's privileged background. I went round to see him, his wife answered the door. Elizabeth, is an attractive woman but because of their class difference has something of a sadistic streak to her nature. She had just given Bert his lunch consisting of baked beans followed by rhubarb and prune crumble with fig custard. We ascended the oak–lined staircase of their lovely home only to see the bedroom door fly open and Bert, a look of panic in his eyes, with legs plastered to the thighs, goose stepping across the landing on his way to the bathroom. Lunch was obviously on the move and his insides were bubbling like the suction tube of a Humber dredger. I do hope he made it in time. I decided to curtail my visit and return at a more opportune moment.

And as for my letter encased in Bert's plaster, well fear not I have a copy and please find it enclosed herewith.

With my very best wishes to you,

Yours sincerely,

Dear Sir/Madam,

I felt compelled to write to you again as disaster has struck
once more. The post box, which I always use at the village
crossroads (in front of the off-licence, unisex hairdressers and
tanning centre) has been the victim of yet another incident.
On this occasion it was not so much a problem with the post
box, but with Bert our intrepid postman. Now, when he
arrives to empty the post box he usually parks his van on the
forecourt of the off-licence but this time another van was
parked there. 'Andy's Mobile Disco' it said on the side, 'a
swinging scene for every party, all ages and tastes catered
for.' What made it worse was that the back of the vehicle in
question was just two feet away from the post box, making
opening the door a problem. But as it happened, it was a
problem that was short lived as Disco Andy emerged from
the off-licence, struggling with a case of lager.
"Sorry mate," said Disco Andy, 'er, could you reach into
my pocket and get me van keys and open the back; I've
got me hands full?"

Bert obliged but he had several sideways glances from
passers by as he firked about in this man's trouser pocket.
Anyway, cutting a long story short, he got the key, opened
the door, Disco Andy put his case of lager in, shut and
locked the door, thanked Bert, got in van and, as many
people often are, was summoned on his mobile. Bert
locked the post box and was about to go to his next port of
call when Disco Andy's van and loud in–car entertainment

46

system started simultaneously. To his horror, Bert realised that his jacket was trapped in the van doors and the van was on the move. He banged frantically on the back of the van to no avail; his banging went unheeded as it was one more thump amongst the many–decibelled thumps coming from the music machine.

The van set off along the road: 10mph, 20mph 30mph. Thank goodness it was a built up area, and hooray for speed cameras. After a few minutes the panic had subsided, Bert got into his stride and was able to keep up the pace running backwards. He tried to attract pedestrians' attention, hoping they would phone the police to intercept, but with him running backwards and seeing him pointing to his back with alternate hands they thought he was an advertisement. I mean, after all, it was a disco van playing loud disco music and Bert running backward with jerky arm movements. Well, quite naturally they all thought he was a rap artist. His only chance of attracting the driver's attention would be if he switched off the music and put on the Archers, but that seemed unlikely.

After fifteen miles and fatigue beginning to set in, relief came in the form of traffic lights. A small boy with a skateboard was passing; Bert had a brainwave and offered to buy the skateboard for twenty pounds. The lad, detecting he could make a financial killing, raised the price to one hundred pounds. "Forty," retorted Bert, opening his wallet.
"Eighty" replied the brat.
"Fifty."
"Sixty."
"Done and I certainly have been."

A woman with a child in a pushchair had witnessed this scene, and admonished the boy for taking advantage of Bert's predicament. As the lights changed to amber she snatched her child out of the pushchair. "You can have this for fifty quid," and quickly grabbed the said amount from Bert. Bert gratefully sat in the pushchair just as Disco Andy drove off. What a relief, he could at least enjoy the rest of the drive in some semblance of comfort. What made it more of a relief was that they were now on a dual carriageway and the speed was now up to 60mph.

Salvation was at hand. A police car with lights flashing and siren blaring was approaching. Disco Andy pulled into the next lay-by. The police car pulled in behind. Disco Andy turned off the music. The officer swaggered over and looked down his nose at Bert as he approached Disco Andy.

"Do you realise, sir, that it is an offence to tow a trailer without an indicator board?"

"But I am not towing a trailer, officer."

"Don't argue with me, sir, I have been to college and I know a trailer when I see one, especially one with a dummy in it."

Now I shan't bore you any more with this doubtfully meaningless conversation, but suffice to say that Bert was horror–struck to find that he had lost one of his letters in the preceding mayhem. And yes, you are probably ahead of me in thinking that it was my letter to you. But fear not, I have a copy and pleased find it enclosed herewith.

With my very best wishes to you,

Yours sincerely,

Dear Sir/Madam,

I felt compelled to write to you again as disaster has struck once more. The post box, which I always use at the village crossroads (in front of the off-licence, unisex hairdressers and tanning centre) has been the victim of yet another incident. I hurried up to the crossroads to catch the last collection, but unfortunately as I approached I could see that I was too late, Bert was just getting into his van. But being the kind of guy he was he saw me and waited. At the same time someone else was glad to catch him, it was Sid from the bungalow who was posting a hi-fi stereo system to his grandson for his birthday. The package was rather large and heavy, measuring some three feet by two feet by two-and-a-half feet. A bit of a struggle for him but he eventually got it posted. Mopping his brow he said he was trying to improve his grandson's musical appreciation and had included a CD of Max Bygraves' greatest hits. A fine gift indeed. Pleased with his efforts, Sid went back to the bungalow.

Bert approached, and as he reached for his keys the unbelievable happened. The ground shook and heaved. A huge split in the pavement could be seen approaching us. We stood aside as the ground parted and, to our horror, the post box was consumed by the earth. We looked in awe into the huge crevasse and could see the post box resting on a ledge, some one hundred feet down. Apparently, according to Bert, being something of an authority on many subjects, the village rests on a geological fault line called the village geological fault line. Some experts say it is a little known offshoot of the more famous San Andreas fault. Anyway, we decided to climb down. We reached the post box when to our horror once more the ground began to heave. It was an after–shock and the fissure above us began to close. We were trapped beneath the earth. The tremors made the post box fall even deeper.

After our initial panic had subsided we realised that, far from being plunged into darkness, it was in fact light. Not just light but there was sunshine. Here we were far beneath the surface and there was light and even a breeze. There was water and grass and flying creatures, in fact a world within a world. We could feel that the atmosphere was charged, charged with a sort of unexplainable energy. There was no time to try to understand it, the priority was finding the post box and getting back home. But where to look?

Eventually we found it, and to our astonishment it was standing upright in the middle of a large canoe at the edge of a lake. How had it got there? Then it dawned on us that it had been put there by someone or something. Our blood ran cold. Then, as a sort of reassuring link with reality, we could hear music, and it was coming from the post box. We could only surmise that the energy we felt in the air had somehow activated Sid's grandson's hi-fi and we could hear the dulcet strains of Max Bygraves singing 'You Need Hands'. Our reassuring link was abruptly severed when we heard voices approaching. We hid and watched. Six scantily–clad men and women got into the canoe and started paddling. Three at the front, three at the rear, and the post box in the middle, like a giant funnel, emanating 'You need hands'. We decided to pursue and, finding another canoe, we followed at a respectful distance.

They were chanting "Um-bo-pa, Um-bo-pa," as they rowed, and Max sang on. It seemed the hi-fi sustained some damage in the fall because only one track was played and it was played continuously. On and on they rowed, the post box standing proudly in the canoe. "Um-bo-pa, 'You need hands'. "Um-bo-pa, 'You need hands'" went on mercilessly.

Eventually we reached the other side of the lake and we watched them disembark. They were greeted by another team with a sort of stretcher in which they carried the post box off into the jungle. We hid our canoe and followed. Our hearts fell when we realised we had lost them. Then like a ray of sunshine, we could hear the familiar and reassuring strains, "Um-bo-pa, 'You need hands', "Um-bo-pa, 'You need hands.' We hurried off after them and eventually caught up with them in a clearing with a collection of primitive dwellings. We were conscious of something behind us. We turned and found we were surrounded by a number of very well endowed women. They urged us forward and we were greeted by someone whom I correctly assumed to be the head man. It transpired that his name was Vince, a potholer who had suffered the same fate as us and liked it here so much he stayed and was eventually made their King. His followers had found the post box and decided to make it their totem.

Our time there was interesting but beyond the scope of this

letter to enlarge upon. So our departure came, and blindfolded so as not to reveal the location of this paradise, we found ourselves in front of a rocky outcrop on the hills overlooking the village. The rocks I had seen many times from the road, little realising their significance. We hurried down to the crossroads and to our astonishment found the post box intact and, looking at the calendar in the off-licence window and our watches, we found that no time had passed at all. Had we both endured a simultaneous fantasy? I guess we will never know what really happened. Bert opened the post box, it was empty but we could hear something, something faint but unmistakable, "Um-bo-pa, 'You need hands,' "Um-bo-pa., 'You need hands." Sid from the bungalow approached with a large parcel. "Can you take this, Bert; it's a present for my grandson?" Weird or what? And my original letter? Well I have enclosed a copy, digitally saved in my computer. How fortunate.

With very best wishes to you,

Yours sincerely,

Dear Sir/Madam,

I felt compelled to write to you again as disaster has struck once more. The post box, which I always use at the village crossroads (in front of the off-licence, unisex hairdressers and tanning centre) has been the victim of yet another incident.

The fact is something incredible has happened and I must ask you to be discrete and to keep what I am about to tell a secret. Now I posted my letter to you and there were some workmen digging the pavement nearby. I turned to walk back home when I heard a strange rumbling. Within seconds the post box was launched skyward on top of a jet of crude oil. Yes, crude oil. The aforementioned workmen had somehow fractured a level of bedrock that released this unexpected phenomenon. I say 'unexpected,' but in point of fact there had been a theory put forward sometime earlier by Bert, our erudite postman, that the village was sitting on a reserve of oil. But the man, quite wrongly I think, was considered a crank and his theory discounted. He has, however, been gloriously vindicated.

Now, where oil, wealth and politics are concerned, matters tend to move quickly and this incident was no different. Because of the ever changing price of oil, the utmost secrecy needed to be imposed. The workmen who had made the discovery had to guarantee silence and, to that end, were made a financial offer they could not refuse. They and their families were shipped off to a secret

Caribbean island where they could live out the rest of their days in the ultimate luxury. And to stop them becoming bored they were issued with solid gold, gem–encrusted shovels and picks so that they could dig the odd hole or two.

Meanwhile the site of the gusher was capped and a control valve installed. The oil was quelled and urgent discussions were in progress to decide the fate of the oil. Following geologists' and other experts' reports, it was agreed that the oil reserve was quite a small one, only about one hundred tonnes, in fact it would just fill one ocean–going oil tanker. A plan was formulated. A tanker was to be brought to the village crossroads, no mean feat when you think that the nearest coastline is over eighty miles away. Nevertheless this huge ocean going beast made it. Now, as I have said, secrecy was of the essence because the plan involved filling the tanker, taking it back to the coast and leaving it anchored a few miles offshore until the price of oil rose, which we had heard on good authority it soon would do. The next problem was to keep the oil tanker out of sight, so it was disguised as a hot-dog stall. This brought its own set of problems because certain members of the community complained because they thought that a hot-dog stall was not in keeping with the image of the village and that it would almost certainly attract riff-raff from the council estate. This public outcry was indeed testimony to the effectiveness of the disguise. It was agreed that there would be a round–the–clock security presence, and this seemed to satisfy the dissenters. So the disguise worked and only Bert and myself knew of the secret, and being considered by the authorities as somewhat eccentric, we were not deemed a security risk.

The business of extracting the oil and filling the tanker went on relentlessly and eventually all traces of the oilfield disappeared. The tanker silently slipped its moorings sailed away from the crossroads and found anchorage offshore. All this done and only Bert and I knew about it. What an interesting few days it has been. Life returned to normal at the village crossroads and the oil–covered post box was replaced with a new one. Now as for the price of oil, well I have as much interest in that as in the courtship ritual of the dung beetle.

But what about the letter? I hear you ask. Well unfortunately it became contaminated in the first rush of oil. But fear not, I have enclosed a copy and please find it enclosed herewith.

With my very best wishes to you,

Yours sincerely,

Dear Sir/Madam,

I felt compelled to write to you again as disaster has struck
once more. The post box, which I always use at the village
crossroads (in front of the off-licence, unisex hairdressers
and tanning centre) has been the victim of yet another
incident. Well actually it wasn't the post box but the post
man. Not Bert this time, I hasten to add, as he is taking a
well–earned holiday, but his replacement, Clive. I took the
opportunity of inviting him out for a meal to get to know
him and his wife a little better. Now he is a pleasant man
as far as it goes, but he has a glass eye and unfortunately it
is away been cleaned and polished. The problem was that
one that they had lent him as a temporary replacement was
a little too small and consequently loose. The result was
that every time he opened his mouth it dropped out.
However he had perfected a technique of sticking out his
top dentures and catching it, and 95% of the time this was
successful and was able to reinstate it without anyone
noticing. It is quite a slick technique actually. However, I
found to my amazement in the restaurant that he was not
always quick enough or his mouth was too full to eject the
denture in time and the eye-ball tended to bounce across
the table like a pickled onion. My wife automatically but
ultimately unwisely attempted to apprehend the fugitive
eyeball by stabbing it with her fork, causing it to fly across
the restaurant, whereupon it landed on the table of a party
of high–ranking Saudis. As fate would have it, they were
enjoying their national dish and the glass eye came to rest

in their cous cous, unnoticed by anyone.

One of the group, whom I took to be a very junior minister, picked up what he thought was a succulent goat's eye. Now I cannot describe the sound of the crunch that was emitted as teeth and glass clashed, nor can I do justice to describing the expression on the poor bewildered man's face. I must say, though, that I have to admire him because not wanting to upset his master, he continued to eat this dubious morsel. Not surprisingly, I suppose, he had to excuse himself earlier than the rest. We have since heard that his condition is stable.

Naturally I went over with Clive to apologise and explain, and I must admit the Sheikh was extremely sympathetic and offered Clive a part of his meal as a replacement. An offer which he gratefully accepted. The goat's eye was comfortable, if not a little strange in appearance.

Later on, Clive distinguished himself as something of a hero. Intervening on an attempted mugging on the way home, his appearance scattered the muggers without a blow being exchanged. The victim on the other hand, although probably grateful for being spared the dilemma of a beating, upon seeing Clive, was so distressed that he also took off with great acceleration, and indeed overtook the muggers. In hind–sight I suppose they must have thought he was some sort of Satanist. Oh well, I believe he will have the proper eye back tomorrow.

Now how as this affected my letter to you? I hear you ask. Well I missed the last collection so I bought the letter with me so that Clive could drop it in the sorting office on his way to work. Not strictly allowed I know. However, during the meeting with the Saudis Clive was offered a cigar. No one had a lighter so Clive produced a piece of paper and took a light from the table candle. And, yes, I'll bet you are ahead of me here, it was my letter to you that he used. But fear not, I have a copy and please find it enclosed herewith.

With my very best wishes to you,

Yours sincerely,

Dear Sir/Madam,

I felt compelled to write to you again as disaster has struck once more. The post box, which I always use at the village crossroads (in front of the off-licence, unisex hairdressers and tanning centre) has been the victim of yet another incident. I'm afraid this week I have to report a double problem. The first was with Bert our postman. For want of a better expression 'his head has been turned'. Star struck, to be precise. A very famous and beautiful young film star, whose name protocol forbids me to divulge, was passing through the village, looking for suitable village locations for her forthcoming blockbuster movie. She was accompanied by her producer and as it was a particularly windy day her hair was in some need of attention. So she patronised the unisex hairdresser's, both to have her hair restored and to get the feel of the local ambience.

I arrived for my weekly visit to the post box. By this time word had spread that we had a celebrity in our midst and there was an unusually large queue of people trying to get into the hairdresser's. I heard muffled conversation mentioning Oscar nominations and other dialogue connected to the motion picture industry such as, "I wonder if I can be in the film," and, "I'll bet she's completely different in real life," and other comments of that ilk. I was approached by Wally, our local village idiot, a very pleasant chap with a permanently vacant expression on his face. However, this morning he seemed somewhat more distant than usual. "How are you Wally?" I enquired. "In love," he replied. Naturally I assumed it was with our local visiting celebrity. I was to find out later that was not the case. Anyway, back to the present.

Bert arrived and emptied the box. He was equally unimpressed with the news of the celebrity. That is until she emerged. Now, what happened next was pure Hollywood. Bert stopped mid–sentence as their eyes met across the crowd. There were cries from the crowd of, "autograph please!" and, "is there any truth in the Three–In–A–Bed scandal?" She was completely oblivious to this, only having eyes for Bert. The crowd fell silent and parted like Moses parting the Red Sea as she walked through them towards Bert. "Hello big boy," she said seductively.

I think Bert was deeply affected by this, as he dropped his sausage roll. A little girl with big pleading eyes and a little squeaky voice said, "Can I have your autograph please?" Looking down at her she said, "I'm afraid I have no paper."

The little girl, tears welling up in her eyes turned to go. "No, wait," shouted Bert, "use this." He passed the star the piece of paper and gave her his company issue pen. The little girl, overjoyed with her prize skipped away and as she did so I saw that Bert had given her my letter to you. Bert was indeed smitten.

You will be pleased to know that I have re-typed and re-posted the said letter. But, as I mentioned earlier another problem was to follow. More of that later.

Now I shan't bore you with Bert's nauseating fawning

over this young beauty, but the film went ahead as planned and Bert, despite the star's opening gambit of "Hello big boy," only had a small part. In the film that is. Small, but pivotal.

Bert was to be her husband. The story line was that she was a tough undercover cop and walks in on a heist in the off-licence. She intervenes, shots are fired and the crooks escape, but in doing so they shoot Bert as he is emptying the post box and he dies heroically in her arms. She spends the rest of the movie avenging his death. A brilliant movie I am sure.

Time goes by and the film is completed; we now eagerly await its release and Bert's movie debut. No sooner had Bert filmed his scene the film company moved on. Then we had another post box crisis. Wally, the village idiot I mentioned earlier, approached Bert with a rather bizarre request. He wanted to marry the post box and wanted him to act the bride's father and give the post box away. Bert was naturally taken aback but Wally assured him that he could provide the post box with the kind of life that it had been used to. It would want for nothing. Bert told him that the decision was not in his hands, the post box being company property. Wally was determined and Bert said he would approach his superiors and see what could be done. This he duly did and quite, unfairly I think, they refused point blank. I am afraid big business stood in the way of true love.

When Bert broke the news to Wally he was devastated. Everyone tried to comfort him saying that one day he may find an old telephone box to fall in love with. But all to no avail. Poor Wally was grief stricken. He became very withdrawn and we all worried for his health and wellbeing. He refused food and spent every spare moment sitting with his one true love, the post box. Bert was especially sympathetic as he himself felt the post box was a part of the family. But Wally was too far gone now.

The following morning our worst fears were realised. Bert and I approached the crossroads and Wally and the post box were gone. All that was left was a note and a ladder. Wally and the post box had eloped. The note said that they could not survive this cruel world alone so had run away to be married and to live happily ever after. I hope they do and I wish them both well. Love has triumphed over convention. Long live love.

However, as you may have guessed, my second letter to you was in the post box at the time of the elopement. I feel sure it will be returned after the honeymoon, but in the meantime please find enclosed another copy.

With my very best wishes to you,

Yours sincerely,

Dear Sir/Madam,

I felt compelled to write to you again as disaster has struck once more. The post box, which I always use at the village crossroads (in front of the off-licence, unisex hairdressers and tanning centre) has been the victim of yet another incident. What happened can only be described as surreal. I had returned from the crossroads and was at the kitchen sink washing the breakfast dishes. Looking out of the window onto the lawn, I was thinking what a glorious day, the sun was shining through the trees, creating a pattern of dappled shade on the lawn. When I looked again everything was shrouded in a thick eerie mist, made all the more mysterious by the shafts of sunlight filtering through. Presently the mist began to disperse and to my astonishment on the lawn was the Post box from the crossroads. But how did it get here?

Ted, our gardener, came running in and was in a very agitated state. "Look see, sir, there's one of those post box things on the lawn." Ted was a good man but a simple soul.

As we looked on, the door of the post box opened and a bright shaft of light was emitted; there was still a little mist about and it gave the impression of a tunnel. Two figures stepped out of this tunnel of light, both clad in tight fitting one–piece silver suits. One of them was an incredibly beautiful woman, and the other a man who I can only describe as dozy looking. "Are they from another planet do you think?" enquired Ted.

It seemed obvious to me that it was some sort of prank, possibly perpetrated by our intrepid postman, Bert, a man known far and wide for his practical jokes. I decided to go along with it for a while to see what would happen.

By now all remnants of mist had disappeared and the odd couple were walking around and looking at the house; they seemed particularly intrigued by the shed. They had a device which I assumed to be a mobile phone which the dozy bloke pointed at the said shed. A red beam was emitted for a few seconds which engulfed the shed. "They're going to vaporise the shed!" screeched Ted. "It'll be us next, I've seen it in the films."

"Don't be silly," I replied, "it's just someone's idea of a joke."

Just then I heard a strange squeaking noise coming from the lane. What's that? I thought. Then I saw old Joe on his bicycle that legend has it belonged to his father and had obviously never been oiled during his ownership. Seeing the sight on the lawn he stopped and looked, always being one to offer advice on any subject you cared to mention, as he was an authority on absolutely everything. The silver–suited couple went over to him after a few minutes Joe seemed agitated and ran behind a bush, leaving the couple with his bicycle, which amused them greatly. As for Joe's sudden disappearance behind the bush, Ted's theory was that he had been caught short, having seen him recently in the post office telling Mrs. Cotton that he was a martyr to his bowels.

"Now that's very strange," said Ted.

"What is?" I enquired.

"Joe, he's very quiet. He usually sings Jerusalem when he's on the lav."

The silver suits turned their attention to the motor mower and started to examine it.

"Don't touch that lever!" shouted Ted "It will…"

CRASH!!!!!!!!!!!

Too late…the mower had gone through the greenhouse. Enough is enough, I thought, and out I marched to give these two idiots a piece of my mind.

"What's your game?" I demanded.

"I am frightfully sorry," said the man, "I shall of course reimburse you for the damage done to your glass structure."

"It ain't no structure no more," corrected Ted.

"Thank you, Ted," I'll handle this. Now who are you, what are you doing and why is this post box on my lawn?"

"Allow me to introduce ourselves, my name is Albert Ross, or should I say my assumed name, as my real name I think you would find unpronounceable. And my assistant here is called T.R.N.A., which stands for Total Robotics Not Applicable, or Treena for short."

"Good morning to you both," said Treena in an unbelievably alluring voice.

"How do lass," replied Ted in his most romantic voice. "I think you're a gorgeous piece of woman."

"Oh, she isn't a woman in the purest sense," said Ross, "she is an android."

"She's a robot?" I said, almost biting my tongue for being taken in by this hoax.

"No, an android," he retorted sharply.

"What's the difference?" asked Ted.

"Well they are totally different. Robots are simple mechanical things, whereas Treena, to all intents and purposes, is almost human, fully functional', and can spit and things. Now as to the second part of your question, we are from another world in a far away galaxy and are on a fact–finding tour of the universe. Our craft, which is able to travel anywhere and in any time dimension, is simply adopting the shape of a post box so that it can fit in with your environment without attracting suspicion."

I almost believed him but sharply bought myself back to reality.

"I see you are a sceptic," he said. "I can prove it, come with us on a short journey."

"Rubbish," I said. But at the same time I was intrigued.

Treena spoke in that rich, alluring, melting voice of hers. "Come with us, Alan, we will show you your heart's desire."

The thought of being with her in the close confines of the post box was an invitation I could not resist. She knew my name, probably my heart's desire as well.

The door of the post box opened and the brilliant light shone out. "Let us enter," said Treena, taking my hand.

"What about the greenhouse?" asked Ted.

"Phone the garden centre and order another one," I said, my mind on other things, "I'll see you later."

We entered the post box, the interior was spacious and space age. Looking up at the letter slot was like a huge screen and we could see outside. I must admit it: I was very impressed. "Where and when would you like to go?" asked Ross.

"I...I...I... don't really know," I stammered.

"A mystery trip then. Lovely, I like a mystery," said Ross jovially, "put in the coordinates, Treena."

"Yes Ross, coordinates in."

"Then let's fly."

The whole vessel pulsated and hummed as Treena pressed buttons on a console. I could see the image of Ted, the wrecked greenhouse and the house on the screen and they gradually faded and were replaced by a streaking starlit sky. If it was a hoax it was a brilliant one.

Presently we landed and what I assumed to be the sound of motors died down to silence. On the screen was an image of lush countryside.

"And where has our mystery tour finished up, Treena?"

"Third century Colchester, Ross, and it might interest you to know that in the time we have just left this site is now occupied by a supermarket."

"Well that's progress, I suppose. Would you like to explore, Alan?"

"You mean we have travelled from the village to Colchester."

"Not just travelled to Colchester but third century Colchester."

Well you are probably thinking how I am going to write to you from the third century? Fortunately, due to fantastic technology I have the means to do it from here. So please find enclosed a copy of my original letter, and please bear with me as I think this adventure may be a long one.

With my very best wishes to you, from third century Colchester,

Yours sincerely,

Dear Sir/Madam,

Well here we are, still in third century Colchester. I do hope my inter-century link is working. I will assume it is and carry on. So, Ross, Treena, and I, and the post box arrived safely. Ross is apparently on a universal space jaunt, travelling around space and time gathering facts and information about various civilisations. He never really explained fully why he is doing this but it seems as though he wants to keep out of the way of his 'harridan' of a mother. She apparently wants him to get a proper job and get married or whatever form of communal bliss they indulge in on his faraway planet.

Here we are and Ross wants to explore. As we stand outside the post box we survey the scene. A rural idyll with the sound of birdsong and water, the wind gently rustling in the leaves. Another sound catches our attention, a sort of metallic clanking. We, or rather Ross, decides to investigate. Walking through the woods we come upon a sort of camp and the metallic sound we heard was sword play. In fact it was a Roman settlement sort of soldier's training school. We watched from a safe distance.

"Were there any Roman settlements in the village?" enquired Ross.

"Well there was an Italian film producer who stayed at the local hostelry for a couple of nights, but I don't think that constitutes a Roman settlement," I replied.

Ross was keen to make contact with these Romans, I, on the other hand, remembered some of my history and was not so keen. But he reassured me that he and Treena were suitably armed and if they got a bit restless they could be suppressed. Against my better judgement I decided to accompany them down the gentle incline to the Roman camp.

It was not long before our presence was detected and three of them, armed to the teeth, swords in hand, approached us.

"A reception party is approaching Ross," said Treena coolly.

"They don't look very friendly," said I.

"Leave them to me" said Ross.

I am afraid he did not instil a sense of confidence in me, but still he greeted them with an accurate, if not exactly flattering salutation.

"Greetings to you primitive Mediterranean warriors."

I felt sure he was not going to get any prizes for tact. The largest of the three very large men, who from his garb was someone I assume to be of authority, spoke.

"'Ere, mush are you asking for a bunch of fives up the froat?"

"Such illogical diction for a primitive life form. Would you not agree, Treena?"

"Affirmative Ross."

"'Ere you three, what have you got on? You look in a right two and eight."

I thought for a moment and couldn't help thinking how interesting that the cockney accent developed so early in our history. I could also see that this centurion chappie was becoming a little annoyed.

"'Arf a mo, I betcha you are spies for that Boadicea trying to cause a pen and ink. Right, I'll sort you out."

He lunged at Ross with his sword. Quick as a flash, Treena grabbed the blade and snatched it out of the Roman's hand, broke it into twenty pieces and dropped the fragments at his feet.

"Aggression suppressor, I think, Treena."

Ross took out a device like a small torch and injected the centurion's arm.

"Lord love a duck, what's that?"

With that the centurion slowly descended to the ground asleep and snoring loudly.

"Don't worry chaps, he's only asleep," said Ross to the two soldiers.

"'Ere Chalky, what's that geezer done to the centurion?"

"Dunno Nobby, but it's shut him up. Do him good to give his north and south a rest."

"Cor Chalky, me plates of meat aren't arf barking."

"Yeah mine too; Let's go have a cuppa while mouth–piece is kipping."

"I say, you Roman chappies, is there anywhere we might be able to purchase items of kit, etc?"

"Over there mate, in the quartermaster's store," said Nobby.

"Thank you very much," replied Ross.

"Any time chum. Just help yourself and sign the book. When you've got what you want come over to the cookhouse for a cup of Rosie Lee and a plate of jellied eels."

Chalky and Nobby departed for the cookhouse.

"What's Rosie Lee?" Ross asked Treena.

"Tea."

"In third century Colchester. Better not tell anyone when we get back."

"Don't worry, I won't," In fact it may yet be some time before I do get back so via the inter–century space link I hope this message finds you as it leaves me. And of course, as I cannot guarantee the security of the post box, I have of course enclosed a copy of my original letter.

With best wishes to you from third century Roman occupied Britain,

Yours sincerely,

Dear Sir/Madam,

As you may remember, Chalky and Nobby indicated the quartermaster's store to us before going for their cups of Rosie Lee. In departing they warned us to be careful of the apples and pears in the store as some of them were a bit wonky.

Ross looked around thoughtfully, he had noticed a gated stone arch. "What is it Ross?" enquired Treena.

"I don't know, let us go and investigate. We can call on the quartermaster later."

I felt a little nervous and would have preferred to call on the quartermaster now and go home before the Centurion woke up, but realising that the transport was out of my control, I decided to go along with them. The gate was unlocked and we entered a large tunnel that seemed to be carved out of solid rock. The floor was remarkably flat: a masterpiece of civil engineering. We moved on, our footsteps and voices echoing around the cavern, our way lit by flaming torches mounted on the wall. It was silent and eerie. After some time we could hear the sound of running water and the faint but unmistakable strains of a harp being played. We had come upon a large open area with a bath the size of a swimming pool and from the wisps of steam, obviously heated. As we looked down we could see the bath was surrounded by exotic statues and the walls adorned by mosaic images of ancient Rome, or should I say in this age, modern Rome. It was an incredibly beautiful place and through my shoes I could detect a warm floor. How much of this innovative architectural engineering has been forgotten in our time.

We heard voices approaching and we hid behind some very large jars which contained wine. The voices became louder and a party of soldiers entered and jumped into the bath. There were shouts of "more wine slave" and "bring on the beef." They were obviously gladiators and officers who had come in after a rigorous day killing each other. We decided to continue our exploration and followed the tunnel.

We came upon another gate and this one was locked. "A piece of heavy gauge wire, if you please Treena," said Ross, and Treena duly obliged. With a few twists the gate was open and we entered a dark large enclosure that smelt horribly familiar, but I could not remember where I had come across it before. I was however soon to be reminded.

Treena whispered to Ross. "Ross."
"Yes?"
"Over there in the corner."
"What? And why are you whispering?"
"There are two pairs of eyes watching us."

Two pairs of eyes were indeed watching us out of the gloom, and the memory of the smell was coming back to my recollection. Ross was his usual unflappable self. "Two large striped animals," he said in a nonchalant manner.

"Tigers, Ross."

"Fascinating creatures."

I was far from fascinated; in fact I was on the verge of filling my pants.

An emergency has presented itself and I hurriedly send this message to you across the centuries. I hope that you receive it and that I will be able to communicate again, assuming of course we make it through this ordeal. Also, hopefully, automatically my original letter is also coming through.

So with best wishes from third century Roman Britain to you,

Yours sincerely,

Dear Sir/Madam,

I had decided that I did not care much for ancient Roman Britain as I stood there transfixed wondering whether I would see the post box at the village crossroads ever again. The tigers had started to walk towards us.

"Stun gun at the ready, Treena," said Ross.

"Ready Ross."

"Then fire."

Two orange beams zapped from their stun guns, which caught both beasts on the forehead and they slumped to the floor in deep sleep. My relief was audible, glad that both body and underpants were safe.

We walked towards an opening and into daylight. It was like a large arena. All became clear. A voice called out to us from behind. " 'Ere, you lot still here?" It was Nobby and Chalky.

"What? Oh yes, we thought we would have a look around. It's alright, isn't it?" said Ross.

"Yeah sure. No skin off my nose; we've just come to feed the tigers," said Nobby.

"Look, the gate's open again," piped in Chalky.

"I'm afraid that's our fault," I explained. "I'm very sorry."

"Leave it out mate, no need to apologise. In fact Chalky left it open last week and the tigers got into the bath house just as the gladiators were having a fashion parade."

"A fashion parade?" enquired Treena.

"Yeah, love it they do–all that dressing up. All that muscle and Mister Machismo malarkey stuff is all show, most of them are all a bit limp–wristed, if you get my drift. Not that there is anything wrong with that, I mean, we are all enlightened, ain't we?"

"We certainly are," said Ross.

"Caused a right pen and ink though. Fur and feathers everywhere."

Nobby noticed the tigers. "Ere what's up with the tigers?"

"Fear not," said Ross, "they are merely sleeping."

"That's all wight then," said Nobby, "we'll leave their dinner in their bowl."

I had to ask the question. "You don't feed them on people then?"

"Nah, that's something we put about to scare the barbarians. This is their dinner."

"Pizza?" I exclaimed.

"Nah, it's a piece of round bread with cheese and tomato sauce on it. It's something this Boadicea tart likes."

"It's a Pizza." I reaffirmed.

"Is that what you call it where you come from?"

I decided not to press the point but just accepted that what I had learned from this visit meant a lot of the history books would have to be rewritten.

At last Ross decided that it was time to move on. We picked up various pieces from the quartermaster and made our way back to the time machine just as the centurion was regaining consciousness. We bade him a fond farewell, gave him some aspirins for his headache and departed from third century Roman Britain.

We arrived back home just five minutes after we had left, such is the wonder of time and space. Ted was still on the phone to the garden centre ordering a new greenhouse.

It was an incredible journey and it was a tearful farewell to Treena. Yes, androids do cry. Off they both went, on to who knows where. I hope we will meet again. I think we probably will. And what of Chalky and Nobby and of course the Centurion, our cockney comrades? Well, I suppose they are somewhere, somewhere lost in the mists of antiquity.

And it's off to the post box, back into the routine and yes, please find enclosed a copy of my original letter, just in case it is lost somewhere in time and space.

With my very best wishes to you,

Yours sincerely,

Dear Sir/Madam,

Well here I am back in the twenty–first century and the problems with the post box continue, but I have to say that this time it is not with the regular post box (at the crossroads next to the off-licence and unisex hairdressers). I went to visit my aged aunt in Arnold Street and popped my letter in the box at the end of the street by way of a change, my thinking being that this post box might be free of disasters. How wrong could I be, as I will explain. I'm afraid I must warn you that my tale is both distressing and distasteful.

Now Arnold Street at first glance looks like a typical street of early twentieth century terraced houses, inhabited by mostly mature residents like my aunt. The outward tranquillity, however, held a sinister secret; it was the Phantom Hound of Arnold Street. The usual postman of this area was Clive. You may remember him, the one with the glass eye and loose top set. I had heard of the rumour of the hound from Bert, who had obviously heard it from Clive. According to Bert, Clive had only recently returned to work after being suspended over a disciplinary issue. When Bert asked why he was suspended he was told he was late for work because he was taken short on his way and had to make use of a public toilet. A bit harsh I thought. But the management suspected lead swinging when, after arriving four hours late, he claimed that there was no toilet paper in the lav and he had to sit there until his bum dried. This excuse did not wash with his boss;

in fact it didn't wash with anyone as there was no soap either.

But let us get back to the phantom hound. I arrived at my aunts on a very warm and sultry day, and sure enough, the hound had been. Outside in the middle of the road was a huge deposit. Apparently the hound itself had never been seen but had always left its messages in the middle of the road, which was slightly less unpleasant than on the pavement I suppose. This deposit was uncannily large. I thought of it as one of the foothills of the Himalayas, mainly because it was about twelve inches high.

As I sat in my aunt's sitting room I could observe the Hound's deposit through the window, and in the afternoon heat it began to change colour. It progressed from light brown to mid brown to dark brown to nearly black. Later it rained and the process reversed from nearly black to dark brown to mid brown and finally back to its original shade. I had noticed that a lot of the houses in the street appeared to have been rustic rendered but according to my aunt this effect was caused by a local boy racer who liked to drive his car down the street at speed solely to drive through the deposits, so producing a tidal wave of you know what. He used to wait at the end of the street in his black–windowed car, and if he saw one of the old biddies walking his lights would go on, his engine would rev and with a screech of tyres he was away. It was a distressing sight, seeing a pensioner moving at full kilter on a Zimmer frame, trying to flee the inevitable cascade. And true enough, many of the walls had partly faded silhouettes of these poor victims.

It was time to take my leave, and out on the street I could see that the Phantom Hound had again paid a number of visits.

Four doors down lived a very pretentious and middle class family called Mr and Mrs Biggins-Lately, Courtney and Avadna. They had a large posh car which was always parked facing the wrong way so Mrs Biggins-Lately had to get out into the middle of the road. After returning from a shopping trip they failed to notice that they had parked inopportunely. Alas, Avadna had fallen foul of the foul and in the pile was an elegant gold open–toed ladie's shoe that was being engulfed by the morass. One can only guess at poor Avadna's distress as she must have felt it ooze between her toes. I bade my aunt farewell and went on my way.

Behind me I heard a screech of tyres and the mysterious boy racer sped past me. Thankfully I was not his chosen target. When I got to the end of the street I saw a rustic rendered silhouette on the wall of a postman holding a letter aloft. I can only assume it was my letter. But fear not I have in the time honoured fashion enclosed a copy and please find it herewith.

With very best wishes to you,

Yours sincerely,

Dear Sir/Madam,

I felt compelled to write to you again. The problem this time was not so much with the post box (at the village crossroads next to the off-licence and unisex hairdresser's) but with well–intented but badly executed DIY. Against my better judgement I had volunteered to do my sister's decorating as her husband had neither the inclination nor the skill, and I'm afraid I was only one point ahead of him. However, blood is thicker than water as they say, so I was employed. The reason for this great fervour of home improvement was because they wanted to move and obviously their present property is going to be easier to sell if it is in pristine condition. Now, not only did she want the living room papering but she wanted a carpet laying as well. I had foolishly told her I had fitted a carpet in our box room which impressed her greatly, unfortunately I omitted to tell her that it took me three days and I had to order another roll as I had cut it too short. The project was not without trauma as I shall explain.

I arrived at my sister's early on Monday morning. Her husband was at work and she was just leaving to take Laura, my niece, to school. A charming little girl, but this morning she seemed a little upset about something and naturally I put it down to Monday morning blues. They departed and left me to it. The materials were all there it was just a matter of application. There was a little clutter about but nothing to give me problems. No more than a day, I thought optimistically. Work progressed well and by early afternoon the wallpaper was up. It was a tricky pattern to match up but I think I rose to the occasion very well. A cup of tea, I thought, and a stroll to the post box at the crossroads (next to the off-licence and unisex hairdresser's) to post your letter. I was suddenly caught with a cold sweat of panic as I felt for the letter. It was in the breast pocket of my overalls, that I was sure, but it had gone. I looked in horror at the bird of paradise above the fire place as it stood upon an embossed rectangle in the wallpaper. It was the letter. It must have fallen out of my pocket when I was pasting. Oh dear, the paste is dry. The only thing to do is a strategically positioned picture of the Algarve over the protrudence and hope big sister doesn't notice until she moves.

The need to go out alleviated, I decided to crack on with my next task of fitting the carpet, and here I encountered another, more distressing, problem. Again the work seemed to go well. I was rolling out the carpet and there was a towel on the floor, as I struggled with the roll I just swept it away without really looking at it. The job was done and I was well pleased. Time for a treat of a well–earned Mars bar, I thought. But another disappointment befell me. My Mars bar had gone. It was in the same pocket as the letter and I knew it was still there when I discovered the letter was missing. I looked in despair at my perfect carpet fitting only to see an unsightly bulge in the middle. It must be my Mars bar; it must have fallen out when I picked up that towel. Well I wasn't going to rip up the carpet for that, so I got my large mallet from the tool bag and hammered it flat. Unfortunately a stain was coming through from the Mars bar but I thought, put a chair over it, Sis will never notice.

A few minutes later the door opened and in she came. She was well impressed with what I had done and went to make a celebratory cup of tea. She shouted through "Can I have a bite of your Mars Bar?" I was puzzled, and then remembered I had left it in the kitchen. I was even more puzzled and my puzzlement turned to horror when she came in with an empty hamster cage. "Oh no," she said, "Hector has escaped, Laura will be very upset."

I felt terrible, as you can imagine. I could not confess to battering the poor creature flat. Then I had a brainwave. "I know, I said, I will go to the pet shop and buy an identical one to replace him." She gave me a photograph of the demised creature and off I went. Luck was in and I got a hamster that was identical and was back at the house just before Sis and Laura returned from school. I put the creature in its cage and put it back in its usual place. Sis and Laura had just driven into the driveway. I saw through the window that Laura still looked very unhappy, and had on the same sorrowful expression as when she left this morning.

Suddenly sorrow turned to rapture as I heard Laura half crying and half laughing. What is wrong I thought? Has she noticed it's the wrong hamster? "Oh, Mummy. Oh, Uncle Alan, it works it works."
What had worked? I wondered. I was puzzled, and not for the first time today.
"What works, sweetheart?" enquired Sis.
"The wishing well, the wishing well we have made at school in art and crafts."

We looked at each other, puzzled.

"A wishing well?" I ventured.

"That you made at school?" continued Sis.

"Yes, yes, it's wonderful and it works," said Laura, enthusiastically.

"A wishing well that works, how lovely," chirped in Sis, half humouring and half (and this is a word I don't use lightly) puzzled.

"Hector was dead when I got up this morning. I left his poor cold body lying in state under a towel in the living room, now he is back alive. Hooray, how wonderful."

It was indeed wonderful. I decided to collect my tools and return home. What a strange catalogue of events have unfolded today. And what about my letter? I hear you ask. Well there it must remain behind the wallpaper, underneath the bird of paradise. But fear not I have a copy and please find it enclosed herewith. And as for Hector the first, well I hope they move to their new house before too long.

With my very best wishes to you,

Yours sincerely,

Dear Sir/Madam,

I felt compelled to write to you again as disaster has struck
once more. The post box, which I always use at the village
crossroads (in front of the off-licence, unisex hairdressers
and tanning centre) has been the victim of yet another
incident. I was a little late getting up this morning owing
to a heady night of sampling Uncle Harold's home made
beer. A man of many talents of which beer brewing is one
of his most popular. I awoke not so much hung over a
woolly minded, and I walked up to the post box with a
slower than usual gait and a slight grin on my face.

Upon my arrival at the post box I realised I was too late for
the collection as Bert had just emptied the box. He did
offer to open it again, which I think is probably against
regulations, but I declined the offer as the next collection
would suffice. We chatted for a while but our convivial
conversation was cut short by the sound of an approaching
commotion. Coming in our direction was a road sweeping
vehicle travelling at its maximum speed of fifteen miles
per hour. We could see the driver running behind it
shouting and waving his arms. We were puzzled at first as
to what was going on and naturally we thought the vehicle
was running away on its own. Then as it got closer we
could see that it was being driven by three rabbits. The
road sweeper was being hijacked by three rabbits, or
should I say by three men dressed as rabbits for reasons
best known to themselves.

The driver was flagging in his pursuit and had decided to give up the chase. The sweeper continued at its breakneck pace, swerving over the road and mounting the pavement, scattering the villagers. In her panic old Mrs. Rogers had dropped her shopping and the sweeper, driven by the laughing rabbits, simply swept it up.

The vehicle was now on a collision course with the post box and impact was imminent. The post box groaned and cracked as it went over and a solitary letter, my letter, was unceremoniously sucked up inside the machine. Bert's sense of duty and courage was magnificent. Without a thought for his safety he leaped onto the speeding vehicle. It had a ladder at the rear of the vehicle for gaining access to the top. He began to climb up. I thought to myself that although Bert was incredibly brave he would be no match for three desperate rabbits, so, still feeling the benefits of Uncle Harold's home brew I joined the fray. I ran after the vehicle and leaped onto the same ladder.

I joined Bert on the top of the vehicle as he was considering what action to take next. The events were to be decided for us. The rabbits, now aware that they had intruders on their hijacked vehicle, were to take evasive action and two of the three were climbing out of the cab and onto the top of the vehicle to engage us. It was indeed an awesome sight to see two six foot rabbits approaching.

A scuffle then ensued and Bert and I were locked in combat with the rabbits. Blow and counter–blow took place. We were wrestled to the top of the vehicle then we in turn had the upper hand. This went on for some time with the driving rabbit swerving the vehicle when he thought it would help his comrades. We were now off the beaten track, going down a narrow lane. Bert lost his grip and was slipping down the side of the vehicle. He was holding on by his finger tips and the rabbit in the spirit of a true rotter, stamped on them. Bert slipped to almost certain death when by fantastic luck his braces became caught on a hook. The driver looking in his mirror could see Bert dangling, so moved to the right hand side of the lane to scrape Bert off against the hedge. Poor Bert was being really battered by the hedge as the driver laughed. But now I had two rabbits to contend with.

As we rounded a bend in the lane there was an oncoming tractor. The rabbit took evasive action and swerved over to the left hand side of the road. This action was threefold lucky. Firstly, a collision with the tractor was avoided, Secondly, Bert was out of the hedge, and finally, the sudden swerve made the two rabbits fall off the top of the sweeper and into the trailer of the oncoming tractor which, by poetic justice, contained fresh manure.

The remaining rabbit, realising what had happened, took desperate action and was now driving and bouncing across country. We held on for grim death. He obviously knew the area as we were heading for the sandstone quarry which had a sheer drop. We feared the worst. Twenty feet from the precipice the rabbit jumped out and legged it across the field. I saw old farmer Brassington in the distance with his shotgun and new spectacles acquired from his late father. Not believing his luck at seeing a six foot rabbit on his land, he let fly with both barrels. It was not a fatal shot; the rabbit was still running, clutching both buttocks. Upset at missing his quarry, the farmer despatched his faithful old Labrador in pursuit. Perhaps he would have better luck.

Anyway, back to our problem. We were approaching the cliff edge and simultaneously with a knowing glance at each other we decided to jump off the vehicle. We rolled in the grass as the road sweeper went over the edge. We watched it tumble down and in Hollywood tradition burst into flames at the bottom of the quarry.

Our adventure over, we decided to revisit Uncle Harold to check out his home brew and steady our nerves. Fortunately the incident was over without loss of life and the rabbits were never heard of again. The village has a new post box and a new street sweeping vehicle but alas, you will appreciate that my letter to you perished in the flames. But fear not, I have a copy and please find it enclosed herewith.

With my very best wishes to you,

Yours sincerely,

Dear Sir/Madam,

I felt compelled to write to you again as disaster has struck once more. The post box, which I always use at the village crossroads (in front of the off-licence, unisex hairdressers and tanning centre) has been the victim of yet another incident. Well actually, it didn't really involve the post box this week but one of our more colourful and eccentric residents called Nigel

Now Nigel was a bus driver who loved his job and not only his job, but also his buses, and he loved them with an almost unhealthy passion. He had in his possession a number of coaches which he was restoring, and there was one that was special of which he had a great scheme planned. This object of his affections was a seventy–six seater, double–decker Leyland Atlantean bus, the existence and ultimate mission of which was a closely guarded secret. A secret which I am proud to be part of and able to share with you. To say his plan was going to be a revolution in public transport would be a most inadequate understatement. Nigel's goal was to bring global and eventually interstellar travel on a budget to the masses. Allow me to explain. I shall start this wonderful story at the beginning.

As I have mentioned previously, our village is blessed with a particularly large and beautiful lake, in the middle of which is a wooded and mysterious island. It also boasts a small pier and robust boat house. I had arranged to rendezvous with Nigel at the lake side. Secrecy was of paramount importance, so this meeting was at sunrise and what a beautiful sunrise it was. The shafts of sunlight, coming through the trees and giving the surface mist on the lake an almost surreal air. A group of ducks quacked in anger as one of their brothers made an inaccurate landing amongst them. I waited in the cool morning air. Where was Nigel? I heard a rustle in the undergrowth and a startled rabbit made his exit. The edge of the lake was bordered with tall rushes and as I looked, they parted and in the quietly lapping water a small boat emerged. It was Nigel. He pulled in and jumped ashore. After a short greeting he bade me get in to the boat and he pushed off. We were heading for the island where he assured me that I would see things most wondrous. It was many years since I had been to the island, the last time I think was when I was about twelve and a group of us spent a balmy weekend camping there, only coming ashore to get fish and chips and a clean change of underwear.

We rowed into the boat house and secured our vessel. The structure, although quite old, was in good condition and at the end the old wooden doors that covered the waterway leading to a long–derelict mansion house looked new and very substantial. I asked Nigel the reason for this.
"All in good time," he said.
Once the boat was secure we walked along the bridle–way to the centre of the island. After about ten minutes we reached the site of the old mansion house which looked as though a lot of restructuring had gone on. We entered, and Nigel led me down into the huge underground cellar of the building. There I was amazed at what I saw. The scene

was almost space age; in fact it was space age, with banks of computers, monitors and a myriad of other technological wizardry. I was in awe and impressed. In centre stage was Nigel's double-decker bus looking just like a double-decker bus. Most intriguing, I thought.

The vehicle was just like the many I had seen before but with a few modifications. Some of the windows on the upper deck could not be seen through and at the rear was a huge propeller. I thought I needed some explanation and Nigel was most enthusiastic in giving it to me. Now I shan't bore you with the technicalities, but the outline of his plan is like this. Nigel, using local business sponsorship, had adapted this vehicle for flight, using a combination of high and low technology. The bus was equipped with concealed floats that made it stable on water. Although capable of flight it had no wings, depending solely on the fantastic aerodynamics of the propeller both for propulsion and manoeuvrability. The power for this initial propulsion was steam. Once above cloud level the upper deck windows, which transpired to be solar panels, would engage. These powered an energised ionisation rocket system which gave an unlimited fuel source for space travel. The possibilities were very apparent.

Nigel told me that the work was complete and it only remained to give it a test flight to prove to the world its commercial viability, and I was to accompany him. He assured me all would be well and that the vehicle had been tested in a vacuum environment and was completely airtight. This was something that worried me slightly as I could see he had kept the concertina double doors and the original driving seat, which was now a pilot's and dare I say it, astronaut's seat.

We both got aboard and Nigel got into the driving seat. The vehicle's original diesel motor had been removed and in its place was housed the steam turbine and boiler. This was the low technology end, though the last word in engineering in its day. We moved forward, down a ramp and onto the waterway that led to the lake. The doors of the boat hose opened and I could see the early morning daylight on the lake. We emerged into full sun, and Nigel taxied the bus to the far end of the lake and turned to face the length of the lake. He instructed me to strap myself in and to hold tight. This I duly did. The mighty motors burst into life and we were hurtling down the lake at a ferocious speed, the wake of the water gushing down the outside of the vehicle, the windscreen wipers at full kilter. What a sight it must have looked to the fishermen at the edge of the lake: a double decker bus hurtling across the water. I could feel the unmistakable feeling in my stomach of take off. I could also see with some apprehension the trees at the end of the lake. My life flashed before me as we just cleared them.

We ascended rapidly in a spiral trajectory. It was an amazing sight looking down on the lake and the village. I unclipped my belt and went to congratulate Nigel. "What an achievement," I said.
"My life's ambition realised," he replied.
We continued to climb until we reached the limit of the earth's atmosphere. We had entered outer space and the steam turbine had been shut down. We were now running on a solar–powered, energised–ion rocket system whose range was limitless.

I was also aware that I was weightless and could swim through the lower deck. Then, feeling more adventurous I floated up the stairs to look at the upper deck. It was a wondrous sight looking up at the stars and then down to our blue fertile planet. Alas, the adventure was too short–lived as Nigel summoned me back downstairs to prepare for re-entry.

I strapped myself in as Nigel manoeuvred the bus to get the correct angle for re-entry, a very critical procedure. We hit the atmosphere with a bump and we were hurtling earthwards. Nigel was using the same spiral technique so that we could land at precisely the same point as take off. As we approached the glide path to the lake Nigel noticed that we had lost a door mirror upon re-entry and that one of the side windows was cracked. Not a major problem, he assured me. The lake was straight ahead and Nigel lined up for landing. We were down, a perfect landing. We taxied into the boat house and back to base. What an experience and what potential. The only set back was that I have lost my letter. I was going to post it on my return to earth and it would have the unique honour of being the first letter in space. The only thing I can think of is that it must have floated weightlessly out of my pocket and been sucked out of the crack in the window. But fear not, I have a copy and please find it enclosed herewith.

With my very best wishes to you,

Yours sincerely,

Dear Sir/Madam,

I felt compelled to write to you again as disaster has struck once more. The post box, which I always use at the village crossroads (in front of the off-licence, unisex hairdressers and tanning centre) has been the victim of yet another incident. The problem this time was a potentially catastrophic natural disaster, the sort of disaster that you would not expect to befall a village such as ours; but befall it, it did.

I think I have mentioned previously the fact that the village lies on a geological fault line. Well at the weekend I was walking the hills above the village and looking down on the lake below. Beneath my feet was a rocky outcrop and I could feel it vibrating, I could feel the tension in the rock. I stood back a few feet, and just in the nick of time, as the rock I stood on split and a jet of steam shot skywards. The phenomenon lasted for about five ear–splitting seconds then subsided as suddenly as it started. I was stunned, stunned and amazed and not a little relieved. Had I not stepped back I could have been poached. I'm sure you're as relieved as I was. That said, I knew something was amiss and the only person I knew who could do something about it was Bert, our intrepid postman.

Bert duly investigated and he was worried. "The signs are not good," he said, and went on to say that this was too big a responsibility for him. He had a cousin, however, called Rupert, who was a professional Volcanologist and had been all over the world studying volcanoes and similar hot spots. According to Bert, Rupert was the best in his field, but alas, he was the black sheep of the family. He was a serial polygamist. It was common knowledge to all except his six wives.

For myself I can never understand anyone wanting more than one marriage with, one would assume, all the incumbent problems that go with it. But Rupert's job took him all over the world, and apparently he balanced the six households perfectly. To look at you would not think of him as a ladies' man. (Indeed what does a ladies' man look like?) In fact he looked quite dozy, with large, very thick glasses. He did, however, show a sort of cold cunning in the fact that all his six wives were called Beryl. This avoided the chance of becoming confused and calling any of them by the wrong name. Not only that, he married each of them on the anniversary of a famous volcanic eruption so he would not forget their wedding anniversary. There was Etna in Edinburgh, Vesuvius in Cleethorpes, and Pittspiloo in Rotherham, etc.

He arrived and surveyed the scene, took readings and analysed data. Bert's first suspicions were confirmed. The hills were about to become an erupting volcano and it was going to happen very soon. Various scientific institutions were contacted but they all dismissed the findings, saying volcanoes in our country are an impossibility. We contacted the local emergency services to put them on standby for the disaster. Again we received a wall of non–cooperation.

The situation looked dire. We were on our own and we had to handle it. Rupert's preliminary calculations revealed where the eruption and consequent lava flow would emanate from. We all shuddered when we saw the results. The eruption, although it was predicted to be small, would indeed send a river of lava straight through the centre of the village. What were the three of us to do? Bert had a brain wave. The boss of the Acme Concrete and Garden Gnome Company owed him a favour. If we could convince him of the eruption and combine it with a business deal the village could be saved. So said it was organised that a concrete channel was to be built in the predicted path of the lava, at the end of which the entire resources of the Acme Concrete and Garden Gnome Company would be waiting.

The plan was completed in the nick of time because at the stroke of midnight the volcano erupted and lava cascaded down the hill. Sure enough, it went exactly where Rupert had predicted. The lava flowed down the channel and at the end was a fleet of concrete mixers which were being filled with the molten lava. As soon as they were filled they sped off to where customers had been offered cut–price concrete driveways, etc, to be delivered whenever a very special consignment of material, was available. The lava was that material and the lucky customers would awaken to a granite effect driveway. Not only that, the Acme company had on site all their flagstone and gnome moulds which were rapidly being filled and shipped back to the yard.

Everyone worked furiously and within an hour the eruption was over and not predicted to return for a thousand years. The village at large was completely unaware of the eruption and if they had heard the noise they simply put it down to the Rugby Club's annual bash. The village was saved without loss and even a bob or two was made out of the lava gnomes and flagstones and of course, the lava driveways. Although I said there was no loss or damage, I'm afraid there was one victim and I'm afraid that victim was my letter. You see, I was to be honoured for my part with a commemorative gnome; actually I don't like gnomes so I opted for a commemorative Buddha. Unfortunately, as it was being cast my letter to you fell into the mould, so it is within the Buddha, I'm afraid. But fear not, I have a copy and please find it enclosed herewith.

With my very best wishes to you,

Yours sincerely,

Dear Sirs,

As I was walking to the post box I passed by the lake and was amazed to see in the middle of it an eighteenth–century sailing ship, and a man–of–war at that. I quite naturally took it to be Nigel, our resident inventor's latest project. I had to investigate. I walked to the pier and rowed across to Nigel's island. Passing the ship I was indeed impressed, the attention to detail was impeccable and the cannon on two decks looked real. The vessel was at anchor and deserted, bobbing gently on the water, its name emblazoned on the bow: Bellrigadon. If Nigel wanted a crew I would be the first to volunteer.

I secured the boat at the island jetty and strode through the woodland to find and congratulate Nigel. Nigel, as you will probably remember, had a laboratory–come–workshop beneath a deserted mansion on the island. As I walked through the woods I was conscious of another presence, and I must admit I felt a little nervous. I stopped and listened. Silence. I walked on. Ahead of me the path widened into a clearing then, after ten yards or so, the path continued through the woods. When I was halfway across the clearing four figures stepped out of the undergrowth and stood before me. I stopped dead in my tracks, fear and confusion racing through my mind. I turned, half thinking of dashing back to the safety of the boat. But my escape route was blocked by another six figures.

The ten slowly approached. They stopped and studied me. I studied them and could not believe what I was seeing. The group consisted of six male and four females. At first glance my overriding impression was of perfect specimens of physique. I thought of the ship, then of their clothing, and considered that it was all innocent, they were making a film. They were dressed as eighteenth–century seafarers as would befit an eighteenth–century sailing ship. Semi relief, I thought. But then something wasn't right. They all dressed the same and they all looked, nearly the same. As I've mentioned they were all very physically well endowed. The tight fitting, clinging brown trousers they all wore emphasised that point and showed off every curve and contour to perfection. And I have to say their thigh–length leather boots certainly led the eye. Around the waist was a thick belt carrying a long bladed cutlass. Each had a short–sleeved leather shirt, which again was sheer and skin tight and had a long, plunging neckline fastened with leather string, which I must admit flattered both manly muscular chests and hugely ample bosoms alike. My feeling was one of fear and the need of a cold shower. A final point about their striking appearance was their faces. They were all fair haired and fair skinned and you could describe both sexes as very attractive. The only abnormality was their eyes. Their eyes were jet black. No whites, no colour, no nothing. Just jet black eyes.

"I am Kara," said one of the women, in an unbelievably sexy voice. She was probably the most attractive of them all, if any difference could be detected between them. Her lips seemed fuller than the rest and as for the size of her chest, well it looked as though she had two fifteen–millimetre rivets sticking through her shirt.

"We have need of you in our world," she continued.

I was flattered, but I thought it would take a better man than me to give her what she wanted; besides I had an appointment at the dentist's tomorrow. I insisted I would not be suitable, which I don't think they really accepted, then made a move to depart. One of the men stood in front of me. I stared deep into his black eyes. I swallowed and he stepped aside, much to my relief. I walked two steps and he spoke.

"We will take you."

I froze for a second.

"Come, Kye, we have much work to do," said Kara.

Relieved, I walked on, thinking that I must find Nigel to see if he had an explanation. I also needed access to the shore as I certainly did not want to come back this way.

With great relief I staggered into the great hall and shouted for Nigel. I heard his voice from the workshop. I hurried down. I hastily told him my tale but he already knew of these people and was formulating a plan.

Apparently, according to his research these people were called the Bellrigadons, after their ship. They are eighteenth–century seafarers, not pirates as such but certainly ambitious colonisers. The legend has it that they tried to take a small south sea island but had made a bad choice as the natives were all witchdoctors and were very much into magic and related activities. They banished the Bellrigadons to a sort of eternal time and space limbo. The curse, however, had a proviso that every fifty years they could materialise at a point and time of their choice and if they could persuade enough people to go back with them the curse would be lifted. Good for them but not so good for their victims. They were given a sporting chance by the witchdoctors by being endowed with superbly attractive features so they could lure victims of both sexes. However, they also had those strange, but not necessarily unattractive, black eyes. The fact that the Bellrigadons were here again meant that they had not yet succeeded in their quest.

"What can we do?" I asked Nigel.

"Well clearly it is up to us to get rid of them because they are going to try to take us back with them which they can do in two ways."

"Dare I ask what two ways are those?"

"Well you could agree to go willingly…"

"Or."

"Or they could kill you and you would go anyway. You wouldn't be dead as such, just living in the eighteenth century, which of course may appeal to some folk."

I'm afraid it did not appeal to me. "Can we fight them?"

"We can, but we can't kill them just as they can't kill us."

"So what do we have to do?"

"Reading the legend I have learned that as part of the

witchcraft that was to curse them the island witchdoctors used alcohol, probably rum and avocado. In what respect I do not know."

"So we have to fight them with rum and avocado. But how?"

"Fortunately in my greenhouse I have a plentiful supply of avocado. Lucky, eh.' But on the rum front we have a problem."

"No rum."

"No. But I have twenty–five gallons of home made beer."

"So we are to do battle with ten Bellrigadons armed to the teeth with cutlasses and bows and arrows and we are going use home brew and avocados."

"Have faith, you are in the hands of someone who has sent a double-decker bus into space."

That I could not argue with, and Nigel laid out his plan. He had acquired a number of coins dropped by the Bellrigadons and he showed me his findings. He had a piece of tissue paper which he had coated with his avocado dip. Apparently not only was he an inventor he was also an accomplished chef. This piece of impregnated paper was clipped tightly across a simply frame which by means of a catapult had one of the coins fired at it. He demonstrated this a number of times and the coins just rebounded. He then took a normal ten pence piece and did the same and the coin went straight through.

"That is to be our armour," he said.

"Avocado dip?"

"Correct. If we smear the whole of our bodies with it we will be safe from harm."

I was not confident. How could avocado dip stop an arrow or the blow of a cutlass? It was bizarre, but so was the whole situation. Nigel continued with stage two, how to fight back. He had a glass of his home made beer and he dropped a Bellrigadon coin into it. Immediately it dissolved. "It's dissolved" I said.
"Not exactly, it has gone back to the eighteenth century and when we use this liquid on the Bellrigadons that is where they will be going."

My confidence was increasing. Nigel produced his weapons, one for each of us, and also a large tub of avocado dip. We both smeared our bodies with this green paste. We did not look a pretty sight, in fact the nearest, albeit most disgusting description was that we looked like two walking bogies. Anyway, our weapons were similarly protected. They consisted of three two–litre plastic lemonade bottles filled with home brew. The bottles, mounted on a framework with shoulder straps, were connected by plastic pipes to a high powered children's plastic water gun. We put them on and prepared for battle.
As we walked through the woods with our beer guns at the ready it was like one of those commando films and I felt like John Wayne. We did not have to wait long for trouble to find us. As we crouched in the undergrowth I heard in the silence a longbow twang and the unmistakable hiss of an arrow in flight. I knew we had been spotted and it was coming straight at us. What happened had to be seen to be believed, the arrow stopped in flight just two inches from my chest. It wavered momentarily then sped off at forty–five degrees, embedding itself in a tree. This happened

another four times. With renewed confidence we ventured out into the clearing. We stood back to back as from the undergrowth emerged the Bellrigadons, swords drawn. I counted nine of them. Kara was not with them. In a strange way I was sort of glad. I had a soft spot for her and I knew we had to do battle.

Kye, the one who had barred my way earlier and had promised to take me, walked forward and raised his sword to strike. I knew I was protected by the avocado dip but primitive instincts forced me to fire my weapon. A jet of home brew shot forward and caught Kye in the chest. He fell and instantly vaporised as he hit the forest floor. The others attacked at once. I could hear the rattle of Nigel's gun as the Bellrigadons charged into the valley of death. After what seemed an eternity the air was silent except for the sound of the birds. On the ground were nine outlines of the Bellrigadons, a fleeting monument to where they had fallen. A mysterious breeze carried away their last images forever.

"The ship," shouted Nigel.

We hurried down to the pier and boarded the rowing boat. As we approached the ship I saw a solitary beautiful figure. It was Kara. She was waving mournfully, a tear rolling down her cheek. But then another figure joined her. It was Kye. Then the other eight. In a way I felt relieved. They fired a single cannon shot as a salute to the victors. Then the ship and Kara disappeared. A lump came to my throat.

"Better get home and bathed," said Nigel "that avocado dip is beginning to pong."

This I did, and as I walked I could not help thinking what kind of life I may have had with Kara. Oh well, never mind.

As I ran the bath I realised I still had your letter in my pocket, but unfortunately it was contaminated with avocado dip and home brew. I will type another, I thought, but when I got to the computer to my horror I saw stuck in the side was a cannon ball. The final salute of the Bellrigadons was embedded in the side of my computer. I switched it on. I could tell there was not much life in it so I had to finish this letter quickly. And so it is finished. I do hope you have enjoyed these adventures of the post box at the crossroads of which this is the twenty–sixth. And I do hope that I have not been too much of a pain. So thank you for listening to me. I can feel the computer fading now so with my very best wishes to you,

Yours sincerely,

P.S. I would just like to say

So there you have it, twenty–six excuses, one a week for six months solid. At this stage you have to make a decision weather to carry on or to target someone else. With the last excuse I have left it open–ended, so I can have a holiday and pick it up again later if I so desire.

I cannot guarantee success using this technique, but your name will certainly be remembered by the recipient. So good luck.

It only remains for me to thank a lady for being the inspiration for a couple of my excuses, but she wishes to remain anonymous. So thank you, anonymous lady.